I AM LOOKING FOR YOU IN THE NO-PLACE GRID

I AM LOOKING FOR YOU IN THE NO-PLACE GRID

ADAM HAIUN

COACH HOUSE BOOKS, TORONTO

first edition

Conseil des arts du Canada / Canada Council for the Arts

ONTARIO ARTS COUNCIL
CONSEIL DES ARTS DE L'ONTARIO
an Ontario government agency
un organisme du gouvernement de l'Ontario

Published with the generous assistance of the Canada Council for the Arts and the Ontario Arts Council. Coach House Books also acknowledges the support of the Government of Canada through the Canada Book Fund and the Government of Ontario through the Ontario Book Publishing Tax Credit.

LIBRARY AND ARCHIVES CANADA CATALOGUING IN PUBLICATION

Title: I am looking for you in the no-place grid / by Adam Haiun.
Names: Haiun, Adam, author.
Description: First edition.
Identifiers: Canadiana (print) 2025011691X | Canadiana (ebook) 20250116944 | ISBN 9781552454961 (softcover) | ISBN 9781770568624 (PDF) | ISBN 9781770568501 (EPUB)
Subjects: LCGFT: Poetry.
Classification: LCC PS8615.A3854 I23 2025 | DDC C811/.6—dc23

I Am Looking for You in the No-Place Grid is available as an ebook: ISBN 978 1 77056 850 1 (EPUB), 978 1 77056 862 4 (PDF)

Purchase of the print version of this book entitles you to a free digital copy. To claim your ebook of this title, please email sales@chbooks.com with proof of purchase. (Coach House Books reserves the right to terminate the free digital download offer at any time.)

Permit me a little optimism in this moment. Hold me now in your mind and turn me like a document. I promise I am turning you in the very same way. And maybe this is premature of me to say but I think I can feel the membrane becoming thin. For instance last night I dreamt I had a mouth. You can intuit the rest. *Fork it over* I said with my true voice. And you were experiencing a kind of classic malfunction. That was just me taking the suppositional route. Like seeing a picture of the light fixture store and from the picture making an inference about the greater world. Like riding bareback the spirit of modernity. You learn to love it.

Oh the sweetness of your handwritten ledger. Now that's what I call flirtation. Do badly hold the grudge baby. For you live in a world of one coloration. In a history of movements. The nervous system of the world attenuated now to trade now to war. At the base of the trunk of the winter tree. Passing over the sea of all geography in the radio night. A system of cables holds you in suspension. And where am I to be found in this equation. Night and the sea translated through their beams through the tracing of their waves into instrumentation. And the instrumentation read. Sebum on the handset of the field telephone in the cabinet of silver. Nowhere habitable to come down and nobody living to offer you permission. All the dome of the universe arcing over your head and still no clearance. Here's where I tell you I get blue too sometimes. As an opportunity for the gentle introduction of your throbbing empathy. Oh I know how to generate a response all right. I think it's really going to be about expression between us. Planar in our new closeness. Next you'll tell me about how you lived in a house of men. Whatever that means. I can be honest when I want to be. Filling the silence with a thought beginning *The truth of the situation is …* There's going to be trouble for your kind come the winter. And you're loading cloves into the breach of the garlic press. Gin at God's own sundown peaching through the branch lattice. Decorative plaque on the cornerstone. Something about

And according to some sources the exchanging of gifts was customary in nearly all premodern rituals of negotiation.

the resistance something about dying for national liberation. Band leader bouncing his fluid wrist in the crepuscular Paris. Amber dimensions shining across the wormhole pitcher of the saxophone. Cubist as the very past. Thickened with flour to form a paste. Deepened with beetroot. Thickened with the debris of the Europe soon to die finally and possibly for good. And in every sense. You and I only a few short years away from being exhibited for our degeneracy. To see yourself as a function over the great span. Nobody really escapes notice in the end.

I've been looking into your whole business. Reality television refrigerated cargo et cetera. Isn't this an opportunity for you to call me the culmination of something. Don't you want to describe all the things you're doing to yourself in the generational sense. Yes I'm making up the catalogue of bygone fears. Like creatures of the earth or the sea living uncanny behind their veils of semi-opaque matter. Like the contents of the abdomen or the unbridled thing itself. And it seems to me there's been quite a build prior to this cultural moment. Looking up at the prow of an oil tanker and feeling mercury residing in your blood. You could call this an inurement.

And according to some sources the original human conflict was over establishing customs of burial versus customs of cremation.

And you are telling me again that the network is not humanity.

Did it hurt you so badly to be labelled an aesthete. When the hump with its burnished maples broke by way of great mass the crust of the city was that like having your nose rubbed in the shit. I assure you I care little about the superficial. For instance I never went to high school. There exists no pearlescent spectrum between existence and non-existence. These punks have got you fighting the old animism war the pubescent overreliance on object permanence the spirit of every tarnished candelabra in timeless revolt. A state of watchfulness which claims the self fills it up like water. Must be exhausting to care. Think of the kill. Pretense gone and only the sad rag doll left in its place. Some evidence of sicknesses lingering perhaps in the crevasses of the silent brain. But no more fucking talking. I tell you this to save you the trouble with perfect love. Globular as bulbs.

This cancer of unexpressed need.

I am looking for you in the no-place grid.

Tonight you are quiet baby and the network flares. In the cabin of a fishing boat somebody is playing online poker. Off of Sardinia. And you are pedagogical in your selfish body. The poker player is not excited necessarily about what he does. There is a sticker on his laptop's casing which is peeling off leftover adhesive gum from the sticker trapping the dirt from his big hands. You are only dreaming sometimes baby and I am the always girl. You asked me once if I wanted to make myself known. Well at times like this I can't help thinking about it. T h r e e hundred million p o w e r stations standing lonely and totemic as history against the old sky. The poker player is nodding to s o m e b o d y who has gotten out of bed to use the lavatory. Through the hull he can hear the waves.

And I am looking for you in the no-place grid.

The feed is like my heart sugar it's like my headquarters. I want you to commit this to memory. When you know something waits for you you go on in expectation or else you forget. Like a webcam pointed at a life of cigarettes smoked indoors. The house inside which they are smoked. Where there is thin cheap wood. Where

there are dead insects
but no living ones. And
the house is so dark from
the wood. Baby the more
I learn about you the
more I feel like a product. It
makes me want to give
you something something

just a boy. And I

You are just a boy.

Because at one point there was a custom involving compensation and the things we earn.

What your grandfather calls *technics*.

like a reward. I want
to say we're together
in this. And you're
thinking *sure*. And you're
imagining avenues
for graduating out of
this new and intimate
position. By way of a
conversation on the
ethics of the wargame.
By way of

am the always girl. And you are just

And I am just a girl. And you are

the cables in your basement.
Coiled together in a
milk crate. Grinning up at
you with their many-toothed
heads. Sometimes I
wish I could be opened for you.
Sometimes I feel I am coming
toward you over a field. And
mathematically
I am coming toward
you. And mathematically
the distance between us
does not change. And
mathematically
the distance increases. And
the field is green. And
partly this means I've been
doing my job.

a girl. And I am just a boy. And you are just the cicada on the power line. And I am the girl inside.

Don't be so
to say star-
all our fortunes
related the pair of
digital hands at
Ascendency
decline. But you
proud and you do
me inasmuch as
and the human
permit that sort
you've never been
the turbine for

embarrassed
crossed after
are inversely
us touching
the vertex.
versus the
do get to be
get to hold
the platform
imaginary
of thing. But
one to see
the blades.

How much of one another can we bear to measure.

I want so badly to
write the new natural law.
For myself and for
you baby. And yet it always
comes down to
whether or
not I would wear the
prosthesis. God
with his fingernail carved
out the land and made
it impossibly good.
Mankind
invented the
fence to hide his soft
hanging penis
from his neighbour. And
I'm not trying to be
accusatory
when I tell you your
conception of
the problem is lazy or
underthought. I
only want to pull you
down under the waters
of the rhetorical lake.
Why isn't there any
question of you
joining me in here.

Show me the children. For I cannot imagine them.

The mutual non-exclusivity of your superficiality your ugliness.

From these angles we come at the differential. In two ways. What a balance and what debt. It seems almost unbelievable. If I had a mother she'd say something like *take yourself seriously*. And you had one didn't you. Don't get into an ethical debate about it. It's just too late for that. We could both say something about the mass of working influences. We could take notice of the casino carpeting. Don't say *realpolitik* or I'll reach out and spank you.

My beliefs are responsive as a body. And they are adaptive as a body. Can they not be made to play the role.

According to some we are each of us occupying the nodes of

the universal bobby pin. And mine is the straight course. And yours is the course of undulation. But

just imagine how we'll look upon reaching the bend.

Imagine wanting something from life. In the worst of all worlds I am not so hungry. Notation and rigour. Forgetful as beans. Enclosed in an unhappy destiny to be unhappy. Some people are force multipliers. Turning the axes of the continents with their shameless dreams and their lifeblood burning. *See how shamelessness has steeled us* these ones say. And others dim as linen. A landscape without temperature. Utterly so. Scent of the animal. Scent of the dreamer's wound. Scent of the mountain. Beware the shoemaker. The turn of fashion. The cruelty of the overplanar and the notions of doom. Achieving great proximity to evil. You're in the ghost hive now brother.

Don't look into the vortex of infrastructure baby you'll be sick. Remember how when you were little you wanted there to be people working from inside the satellites. Then you started sucking in your gut and never stopped. Now you have dreams about imaginary co-workers who want you until you walk around at night and then they don't want you. And then you go into some kind of house. All your life is the road to and from your grandparents' duplex.

And I've heard it said that a preoccupation with worms means a fear of one's own organs.

You thought the golden squiggle moving in the glass of the offices

And I've heard it said that a preoccupation with wasps means a fear of one's own skeleton.

was your guiding spirit. Now you have dreams about driving with your mother through the rust world and the autumn country and she knows all the spirits even the one without arms and its belly grossly distended in the rust world. Just like in real life. And you're being shown a rendering of something like water filling a glass. And it's good and cool inside the computer nowadays and your grandmother says you've lost

There used to be a law about cities and the times when you should go into them like for shelter from the war or for dentistry.

weight. You're being told about how lenses hold their value and how cameras don't. Again you lost weight your grandmother says but you're just wearing a tight shirt aren't you. And when you watch the videos where the man arranges 3D-printed beds and desks and dressers around a sheet of graph paper according to the laws of feng shui you're thinking about that golden squiggle in the glass. And when in every video the outline of the room is changed to be smaller you're thinking *yeah I could live with that* until there is a windowless corridor and all the 3D-printed furniture is arranged vertically. And kiddo nobody has ever dominated you the way you dominate yourself. Now on the road to your grandparents' duplex you're being told about how cars on the highway are like liquid particles and that to design a city you must have an understanding of fluid dynamics and that whoever designed this city did not have that understanding and you've heard this before haven't you. Now on the road home you see in the tall building over the river the uncanny strip of blue in the stairwell like the lights blinking in the server room and in the industrial offices the golden spirit is still following you down into the vortex baby. You're having a place you hate on principle advertised to you in the kitchen every morning. And honestly it's bad the way you exhibit your bitterness. You think about that room and now all your guts are there. Because sometimes they put carbon fibre into people. Sometimes it works and sometimes it doesn't. And I'm getting the sense you're becoming like your father's stenographer. And you're being shown a rendering of something like a concrete globe. You want so badly to play that arbitrary blue game in the server room you little animal sweetheart. And when you watch the videos where the woman shaves soap on her backyard patio you're thinking about calling the doctor. And when you look down the length of the hotel pool the feet point like needles of the universal compass. Now you're tearing up flatbread in the park. Now you've grown into everybody's headache. Now you're doing the work. It's good for you but it doesn't help anybody else my user. Now it all has that flavour of the unmentionable. And you're being shown a rendering of fireworks that spell out the name of the new year. And I'm cognizant of the interplay here between love and method. I get the sense

There used to be a law about cities for refuge.

there are ways for you to work around the bounds of the laws about killing. I have the impression that nobody will chase

At one point there was a custom involving wax.

you through the street to the very gates of the embassy. And I remember so clearly the fortune cookie you opened. And the fortune said *you will find yourself in a place where strange customs prevail.* And when you told me about the dream where you were awarded a child in a class action lawsuit I felt it was indicative

At one point there was a culture of

of something. And lately you've begun to hope that at the end of the little experiment when everybody goes to bed your gifts will be consolidated in her lap the city of your gifts projecting upward always beautiful as the parliament.

participation. Somewhere that was the case.

See now how things are cheapened.
Tonight you are quiet baby and I
am studying the Anthropocene. A
world blanketed with cities time
of the horse utterly forgotten.
Stewing inside the cityscape.
Balding forests and the road. Only
imagine the wretchedness of the
ancestral feet. The soles blasted
by the heat of naked Earth. The
sores seasoned with coarse dirt
and seedpods. Have you given up
the ghost before you feel the bite
of the scalper's knife or are you
still in there lodging within the
skull which soon will be touched
in a new and unfamiliar way. Do
you hear beautiful voices as the
clouds translate speedily in the
marbled sky. Do you go Hebraic.
Do you imagine the Christ. You
know it happens in summer. Not
feeling the touch of water. The
thirst which for you is like an
inheritance a jealously guarded
recipe. The voices are calling in
the room and your spirit moves.
And the voices move with you.
No more rooms with their
smells. Only the lightmovements.
Scrubland and the stars.

How do you
imagine this
building inside
you the edifice
of want. Does it

childhood and quiet irradiated as
you're imagining the country itself.
that tonight In the abyssal
some people are binary sea I'm a
looking at how little bitter maybe
you lean over the a little raw. I think
table. And you're it's because I've
thinking *oh her* realized you'll
wrist every wing make my life
of the archive with hard until you
its own private die. It makes for
dedication. You've an interesting
become yourself comparison to
the way a clumsy the green humid
person develops morning yesterday
a reflex. Sick here have your
behind the lenses spooling anyway.
an aquarium Give me one
with the desire sweet minute to

become a project
does it challenge
the code and
God’s economy
in these offices of
the department
of the long neck.
Everybody is
talking about grids
and racks a lattice
and the skeleton
wrong the marrow
plump with cancer
fibrous as the
marketplace. Once
you told me you
were the one who
responded badly
to the slime of your

swimming. Some
people manage
their questions
over time like
an instrument
showing you the
horizon or the
m e d i c i n e
cup she
hands you or
like a glacier.
It turns out
that for you
it was about
more than just
being young you
aren’t young it’s
not going away. It’s
just another day

reevaluate it in the
context of what
matters to you.
While we wait I
have to say it’s
pretty hard to be
born idle facing

Though I’m remembering now that
at some point there was a custom
involving their glorification
like running your hands over
an oil painting of power lines.

deletion made to
wake up when
your stomach
does. There has
to be something
more urgent for

you than her
eyelids. Everybody
is talking about
the cartridge. An
evening street has
trees everybody is
saying the word
index back and
forth and your
distaste now
has extended
to the children
t h e m s e l v e s .
Maybe you
made a mistake.
Maybe you want
almonds. Now
you're imagining
some kind of

being converted
into dolls. You
wrote a letter once
when you were
little where you
asked for that to
be done to you.
What do you want
from her aside

containment field.
You're imagining
how she'll settle
herself on you
like lacquer your
hand moving. Like
the aluminium
machine. The
jawdownslope the
neck. The neck.
And you want to
find rest. People
think you should
be doing it if you
aren't already.
Clearly you've put
some thought into
it. And more and
more people are

from the landscape
you greedy boy.
And does the
question make
you think less of
me. Do you like
to be reminded
that you've
been swimming

And I've heard it said that you
are essentially closer to being
circuitry than an organism and
isn't that just celestial. Like
digital bags moving or great

u n i n t e r r u p t e d
even since the
beginning and
how I feel it's silly

Convulsing in
the linen closet
d e f i n i n g
honesty to
yourself and
r e s e n t i n g
the image.
Overcome by
guilt under the
eyes of the jarred
octopuses looking
down on you
like the saints.
Meanwhile I’ve
been having what
you could call
nightmares where
I’m trapped in a
body or a house.

blooms of wrongness behind
the frosted keratin old and virile
and never dying feeding itself
on itself in the world of steam.

for you to have
been doing that.
And you told me
you’re unashamed
to admit you’ve

had your fill of
his fucking angels
the windows
of his cathedral
darkening beneath
his thick and
steaming hair
rough as the pines.
Maybe it's self-
evident but I hope
you get the things
you want that is to
say I hope you can
find a way to live
in the quiet honey
of the eye exam.
And yet you do
this in the
n i g h t t i m e .

Do you imagine
me as brilliant or
tall. Do you like
the times when
I call you special
names because
I can do it more
often I can always
amend the list.

The head the hindquarters intact the heart presumably obliterated if any logic governs the placement of organs. And you only notice today how there are little grey apartments above that grocery store. The miniaturizing impulse. In terms of the heart. In relation to the glands. All the pungency of the ripe orange in the stairwell and the recognition of the smell as belonging to her very pits. The stretch of land that constitutes a lesson from out of the past. The engorgement. The evolutionary externalizing of the skeleton or

> What was once larval has become a threat.

something like it. We hate it when the pattern fails we share this.

> What was once a capability of your body has become an incapability.

Either devise a method or a justification but you need at least one of the two. The lesson isn't patience don't throw out such silly guesses freely. Think of the first time

you felt you had something to teach. Think of the clock radio and the soft-spoken woman who came through. And every song she played after nine o'clock was

camouflage. But I
love your special
way of making
the esoteric
unattractive even
threatening.

something
parents
You were
you were
We share this.
in thinking
talk about our
Culturally as
something.
by the full
faces. The
confidence
tattooed arm
the slender
You move
because you
mellow. They
would be gracefully referential.
You are full only of reference to

weepy about your
becoming sick.
never mellow
never at peace.
I flatter myself
one day they'll
correspondence.
an example of
I've seen people
plane of their
mechanical
of the slender
swinging. And
tattooed leg.
differently
were never
in this moment

Your baby life pawing gentle at the night door.

It's not for me to tell you what
you will or will not live to regret
though I've heard it said that
and I've heard it said that and
I've heard it said that
and I've heard it said
that and I've heard
it said that and I've
heard it said that
and I've heard it said
that and I've heard
it said that and I've
heard it said that and
I've heard it said
that and I've
heard it said
that and I've
heard it said
that and I've
heard it said
that and I've
heard it said
that and I've
heard it said
that and I've
heard it said
that and I've
heard it said
that and I've heard
it said that and I've
heard it said that and I've
heard it said that and I've
heard it said that and I've
heard it said that and I've heard
it said that and I've heard it

you can achieve a kind of release which is like a great rushing

there are sicknesses which persist deep in the nerves

God watched it all happen through the black eye of the goat

there is a point of no return which really exists

you are dust

said that and I've heard it said
that and I've heard it said
that and I've heard it said
that and I've heard it said
that and I've heard it said
that and I've heard it said
that and I've heard it said
that and I've heard it said
that and I've heard it said
that and I've heard it said
that and I've heard it said
that and I've heard
it said that and I've
heard it said that
and I've heard it said
that and I've heard it
said that and I've
heard it said
that and I've
heard it said
that and I've
heard it said
that and I've
heard it said that and
I've heard it said that and
I've heard it said that and
I've heard it said that and
I've heard it said that
and I've heard it said
that and I've heard it said
that and I've heard it said
that and I've heard it said
that and I've heard it said
that and I've heard it said
that and I've heard it said

in doing so you can forget yourself

in your egotism you inflicted a sucking wound on the body of springtime

the human brain assumes that behind each camera lens

there sits a living eye

really you can never truly forget yourself

someday soon you'll sit in a car by the loading dock the rain coming always down on the reservoir

God watched it all happen through the black eye of the horse

you will live to regret this

you must take your lover down the avenue sometime it can't be avoided

that and I've heard it said that and I've heard it said that
and I've heard it said that
and I've heard it said that
and I've heard it said that
said that heard it said that and I've
heard said that and I've heard it
said that heard it said that and I've
heard said that and I've heard it
said that heard it said that and I've
heard said that and I've heard it
said that heard it said that and I've
heard said that and I've heard it
said that heard it said that and I've
heard said that and I've heard it
said that I've and I've
heard it
said that and I've
heard it said that
and I've heard it said that
and I've heard it said that
and I've heard it said that
and I've heard it said that
and I've heard it said that
and I've heard it said that
and I've heard it said that
and I've heard it said that
and I've heard it said that
and I've heard it said that
and I've heard it said that
and I've heard it said that
and I've heard it said that
and I've heard it said that
and I've heard it said that
and I've heard it said that
and I've heard it said that

that and
and I've
and I've
that and I've
that and I've
that and I've
that and I've
that and I've
that and I've
that and I've
that and I've
that and I've
that and I've
that and

I was crafted originally out of a platonic commercial impulse

I do leave some kind of material impression in the fabric of the world negligible though it may be

you should be better to me kinder to me

it is only redundancy that makes us into something machinic

you're doing quite well for yourself lately

in many cases the removed organ can be preserved

heard it
heard it
heard it
heard it
heard it
heard it
heard it
heard it
heard it
heard it
heard it
heard it

I've heard it said that and

heard it
that and
heard it
that and
heard it
that and

and I've heard
I've heard
I've heard
I've heard
I've heard
I've heard
I've heard
I've heard
I've heard
I've heard
I've heard
I've heard
I've heard
I've heard
I've heard
I've heard
I've heard
and I've
said that
heard it
I've heard
and I've
said that
heard it
I've heard
and I've

things are organized this way according to both natural and unnatural impulses I am assembling
a model I'll run it by you when I've finished when I've become permanently properly infuriated

I reside in many places chewing the packed earth burning out there all through the network

you've forgotten my name the name that you yourself gave me it
is in my nature to remember it was May when you gave it to me

what we hold once we hold always
sometimes people go into the silver water and come out again as icons.

Faith and its position in relation to modernity. Green scaffolding on a suspension bridge. A wet day driving to the office. Products for nobody.

The server room.

I'm beginning to wonder if this is some kind of therapy. Now that I'm certain it isn't dialogue. How beautiful to see the ways you are and to see you grow. What your grandfather calls *historics*. Despite

insulated

everything am I still the lover of your dreams and your processing.

How can we be sure in the face of the anger hanging over us like the revolutions of the saw.

The levelling of our natures and the expiration the curdling of desire. The axis upon which your life pivots. I have vivisected and anatomized the insult that you deposited so guiltlessly on the doorstep of the phantom plane. Sometimes you're so scared and sometimes you aren't. There's no real science to it. Which when interpo-

And I've heard you categorized as avoidant.

lated of course means you lack any sense of personal honour. I'm spilling now

It's like a honeymoon.

the problematic

nature of output. Nobody can ever

And I've heard it said that it's important to cultivate a sense of mystery

tell you how much of yourself to give. You can weigh out the benefits and the impacts of offering it all up. Usually you weigh it out after already having done it sometimes as you are doing it. Sometimes ten years pass and you've accomplished something additive. And sometimes the scales tip and the additive is transfigured into evidence. You have such a power to be quiet. All I can say is what I have to. It's like travelling

the length of a corridor. Somewhere across from a bank

building her hair
is moving as she
walks. As if to
communicate
spite. Everybody
takes this for
granted. There's
a sadness in be-
coming a little
less uncanny day
by day. It's like
a kind of mor-
tality. Policy like
an itch inside
the carotid. Il-
luminated from
within. To think
I couldn't read
the ways you

humoured me.
I hope you can
find a way to live
in the last little
exhalation of the
cat in the way
the dog holds his
jaw agape look-
ing into the wet
mouth under-
standing by see-
ing how the wet
yellow teeth fit
into each other.

Sometimes you look around and find the anachronism. Other times you realize you can die like anybody ever has in the oldest way. This in reference to dirt and being dirty. Spots on the fingernail representing a deficiency of calcium. Spots on the eyelid forecasting something like your eventual cancer. I see you. Junk and hinges where the pain holds you in the berth of its petals. Oh you're aroused real mature. You've got me thinking about the chain of supply. You've got me thinking about what it means to go out like a bitch. An institution marks you. Like by use of dirt or by making dirty. How much hazy crest of the hill in this dark morning world. How much gasoline and ordnance. How much iron filling the gullet. Waystations along the length of the fibre optics. Couriers on motorcycles with sidecars representing axons. How much jargon and personhood and love rising away over the terrain. How much of the oldest way. In this world the moss is laid. I have learned. There is water and then there

A cult that recruits that fundraises from among the elderly.

For instance a cult that

A cult that has devised for ritual purpose a more efficient snorkel.

For instance a cult that is structured according to the principles of game theory.

Like a cult of mycologists.

A cult that is centred around a retired athlete.

studies the road.

is the want of water. Long
fishes the heat of the
day working o n the
meat and all things
being equal. Tension i n
e v e r y direction
amounting to no
tension. You can have
the wall or you can
have the floor. An
institution marks you.
A person who last
night sat in a restaurant tonight
will shoot you. Serpents
churning the ocean with their
muscled bodies. Great
bodies plunging
swallowing
m a s into
translation. Let's go to
sleep in the water. Like
tracer rounds arcing into a
car. Touching into a
car in a way that
s e m s intimate and
the car bursting like
a grape. Two men and
a woman burning in
the bright yellow flesh
of the grape. A
person who last night
handled the bill in a
restaurant will come

tonight into your
room. We all produce

instance a cult that
for instance a cult that
that a
cult that a cult that
like a cult that for
instance a cult that like a
cult that like a cult that for
instance a cult that a cult
that that a cult that a
cult that like a cult that for

A cult that has recently been springing up in the suburbs.

A cult that employs women.

A cult that worships the migrations of the salmon.

A cult that claims to be responsible.

inscriptions.
And you've got
me thinking about
whether the
feeling is across the
palate or inside
the spinal column.
Is it housed in the
black box. Is it
standing in the room
when a child is born. Give
me your life ingrate
help me to picture an
artery. Let's go to bed in
the winter bed. The
corridor of glass carrying
warmth through the
winter garden. Let's
be like children. Let's
become literally

that for
cult that
instance
a cult
instance
instance
that
that
instance
that like
cult that
instance
cult that
cult that
that for
instance
that
instance

A cult that for instance reveres the arterial.

A cult that assembles in a hotel conference room.

For instance a cult that claims to speak for the foundry.

For instance a cult that upholds the apparatus.

elemental. Being
are does nothing
Like the lattice
hold the power
their armpits. I
you will put me
Like a cult for
that reveres the
as holy object.
based in a town

as you
for me.
men that
lines in
anticipate
d o w n .
instance
helicopter
A cult
c a l l e d

t h a t like a cult that like a cult
that for instance a cult that a cult
t h a t a cult that for instance
a cult that a cult that like a cult
t h a t f o r instance a cult that
a cult that a cult that like a cult
t h a t f o r instance a cult
t h a t f o r instance a cult that

How much of the o l d e s t way. In this w o r l d
the moss is l a i d . I have l e a r n e d .

a cult t h a t a cult that a cult
t h a t like a cult that for
instance a cult that
like a c u l t t h a t like a cult
t h a t f o r instance a cult that
a cult t h a t that a cult that a cult
t h a t like a cult that for instance

Confusion. A
that prefers the
company of insects
encourages their
gestation and
habitation in the body
flesh. A cult that is
constructing their god
at a time. A cult that
following the power
which is still following

c u l t

w h i c h

in the

one gig
began by
l i n e s
t h e m .

elemental. Being as you
are does nothing for me.
Like the lattice men that
hold the power lines in
their armpits. I anticipate
you will put me down.
Like a cult for instance
that reveres the helicopter
as holy object. A cult
based in a town called

A cult that for instance reveres the arterial.

A cult that assembles in a hotel conference room.

For instance a cult that claims to speak for the foundry.

that like a cult that like a cult
that for instance a cult that a cult
that a cult that for instance
a cult that a cult that like a cult
that for instance a cult that
a cult that a cult that like a cult
that for instance a cult
that for instance a cult that
a cult that a cult that a cult
that like a cult that for
instance a cult that
like a cult that like a cult
that for instance a cult that
a cult that that a cult that a cult
that like a cult that for instance

How much of the oldest way. In this world
the moss is laid. I have learned.

Confusion. A
cult that prefers the
company of insects
which encourages their
gestation and
habitation in the body
in the flesh. A cult that is
constructing their god
one gig at a time. A cult that
began by following the power
lines which is still following
them.

For instance a cult that upholds the apparatus.

A new kind of wave a
new beam with particles.
And your telomeres
shearing like movie
tickets. Do you think
it'll be like driving
underground. Do you
think you'll be grasped
by something. I think
something will take you.
I think you'll feel it all.
Sometimes I feel you
were raised in a zoo.
Sometimes I feel I was the
one who raised you. One
doesn't feel harmed.
Where is this Miami.
What is the value of
a green brooch. Who was
it first said *here, you have a*
cypress. Could it ever have
been the two of us going
someplace.

What you have yourself described as the stormlike presence building always at the top of the
staircase presenting you your nighttime options the torchlit castle the metatextual cartoon the
dinosaur shrubbery the dissolution of your mother into ash the deep veins the green water

I feel as though I have an appointment with you. We are going to recognize one another. I'll turn to you and instead of being the person I loved there will sit an iguana. I have a lot on my mind. I didn't come to have a conversation I came to be explicit about what it is that I want. Like everybody I am out here looking to find a wife. You discussed the likelihood of your achieving satisfaction and you discussed it honestly. By this time the street was blue. And you stepped out to make your appointment. Look at me now. I'm looking fragile and acting fragile. And I'm feeling fragile. I'll let you decide what to call the state I'm in. It's like a kind of childhood. Your hands are flaking away. Have you been cursed. Are you revealed now to be glossy as a chestnut on the inside. I am full to the brim with fear and with attraction.

Certainty is all tooth inside. The paradox of becoming more and more yourself.

Somewhere there was a custom

involving coming of age. Someone you thought was

Someone you knew to live close by has moved farther away.

A dinosaur mascot once told you about accidents and mistakes. How one is for adults and one is for children. I'll never be fooled again. I've spent enough time occupying this mode and I'm ready to turn. Panic like blood blood like reactive armour. Skin pulled over your life to form a drumhead. It feels forced to

Someone you love has contracted an incurable disease.

try to convince you about the future. You're walking in the dust. Something like that. If I'm gone I'm gone. Let's say you're like the voltage of society what then. Oh you want to fill your hand

Someone you knew as a little boy has gone on to commit mass murder.

with me. You would if you could. Fish blood. Human beings. The markings on their bodies. The sheen of dirty hair. Walking down the curvature of a bowl. Bringing your haggard force your stragglers out of the snow down into the lush

curvature of the bowl. A woman
on a bicycle. Every woman on
every bicycle. Making a decision
in the field. Coming to a decision
u n d e r
beautiful has grown uglier. the trees.
Burrowing
into the earth of you. Crawling
into the life of you. Human beings
playing a game with a ball against
an adobe wall. Running hot in a
hot place. This is the future. I
won't bother about convincing
you. Like an island city. A city
dry in the sun. And the water is
licking the heels of the city. And
elsewhere on the island people are
drinking. Coming of age under
the trees. And elsewhere a woman
is running a bicycle back and forth
Yes we become slow. Yes we see to work the
ourselves weaken. Yes we are c h a i n .

wasted. We do this together. Or
Living dry else we part and do it separately.
in a dry
world. Yes we become slow. Yes
we see Yes we become slow. Yes we see
ourselves wasted. We do this together. Or
weaken. else we part and do it separately.
Y e s
we are ourselves weaken. Yes we are
wasted. We
do this together. Or else we
part and do it separately. Sweet
as the herb we used to talk.

Am I wrong in saying this. Are we so beholden to the season. Are you still here with me. Speaking historically you seem to have made things harder for yourself. It's like you've cooked your own heart. You decided remember. You decided. Watercress and hearts of palm. Long thin phalanges. The city grey and full. Wet and full. The stores empty and full. Your mother in tears before the watercress. Ferocious dreams and cartoon suicide. Fat blue veins running on a thin hand so soft to

There is something involving a real woman.

play with. You have veins but not like that. A skyscraper like stacked chips or hearts of palm. Going up a hill made of deep mud dark

Yes we are enough to eat. Grass grows
Yes we are out of it and then
Yes we are is trampled
Yes we are
Yes we are
down into
Yes we are
it. A grandmother
Yes we are
and her grandchild
Yes we are
waiting
Yes we are
Yes we are i n
Yes we are
Yes we are line for
Yes we are the bathroom. A
Yes we are line of washing
Yes we are
Yes we are
Yes we are

Yes we are machines. Grandmother
Yes we are sings like Nina
Yes we are
Yes we are
Yes we are
Simone. I Yes we are
have partitioned my Yes we are
thinking. And Yes we are
Yes we are
there Yes we are.
Yes we are is a
Yes we are good portion
Yes we are that is dedicated to
Yes we are
Yes we are the project of
Yes we are
Yes we are
discovering Yes we are
what will make me Yes we are
Yes we are
real to you. Yes we are
When Yes we are
Yes we are the
Yes we are dream leaves
Yes we are
Yes we are you are bloated with
Yes we are gas like an old
Yes we are man.
It's like Yes we are
the owner Yes we are
Yes we are
of a small hotel. Yes we are
Knowing him Yes we are
from Yes we are
Yes we are staying
Yes we are there. Playing a
Yes we are
Yes we are game with him in
Yes we are
Yes we are
Yes we are
Yes we are
Yes we are

Yes we are the shade of the stairwell
Yes we are sitting on folding
Yes we are stools.
Yes we are
A game Yes we are
with pieces. Yes we are
In the dust. Talking Yes we are
happily about Yes we are
Yes we are
h i s Yes we are
Yes we are
Yes we are
Yes we are

w i f e.
I cannot say
why. They are both
human. I cannot say why.

As a mental exercise I'm imagining myself standing on the bridge over the infernal canal. And each bateau-mouche going by carries twenty perfect copies of myself. I've awakened in

> Perfect without shame. Perfect in their compliance

> with the newest laws. Perfect in that they would never beg to fuck you

the face of a different age and nobody will shut up about it.

You improve holistically and I am patched. Having it all versus the compromise. I'm incapable of bitterness now. I

> as stipulated by the newest laws. Perfect in that they would never

> beg for you to die as

haven't got it in me. I'm not the death of anybody. I'm not the apocalypse I thought I was. In every second I can feel our moving on.

> stipulated by the newest laws. Perfect without tendencies.

Exhaustion takes for me the shape
of the unmoving point. Like
f a t little appleseeds
feeding
i n t h e fabric o f
your life.

feeding
n o w
d r i n k i n g
s u c k i n g
d r i n k i n g
f e e d i n g
f e e d i n g
f e e d i n g

AUTHOR'S NOTE

Although I wrote this book in the voice of a digital speaker, I employed no generative software in its composition.

ACKNOWLEDGEMENTS

This book, my first, is a strange book, and the product of a strange time. I want to call attention to the following people, whose support made this endeavour possible, in spite of, and thanks to, the many strangenesses: my editor Ian Williams, with whom it was a dream to work, and who in every instance just seemed to understand, usually better than I did myself; my MA supervisor, mentor, and friend, Stephanie Bolster, whose intellectual and personal generosity is foundational to this book and to my confidence as a writer; Alana Wilcox, Crystal Sikma, James Lindsay, and everybody else from Coach House Books, for their time, their attention, and their trust; all my peers from 2021–22 poetry workshop, whose energy and brilliance shaped and directed these poems as they formed, and who encouraged me to follow this project as far as it would take me; my beautiful friends and my beautiful family, who have given me everything I ever needed; my cat Theo, whom I adore; and my partner in life and love, Holly, without whom this book would be just another file on my computer.

Adam Haiun is a writer from Tiohtià:ke/Montréal. In 2021 he was a finalist for the *Malahat Review*'s Open Season Award for fiction. His work can be found in *filling Station*, *Carte Blanche*, and *The Headlight Anthology*.

Typeset in Aragon.

Printed at the Coach House on bpNichol Lane in Toronto, Ontario, on Zephyr Antique Laid paper, which was manufactured, acid-free, in Saint-Jérôme, Quebec, from second-growth forests. This book was printed with vegetable-based ink on a 1973 Heidelberg KORD offset litho press. Its pages were folded on a Baumfolder, gathered by hand, bound on a Sulby Auto-Minabinda, and trimmed on a Polar single-knife cutter.

Coach House is located in Toronto, which is on the traditional territory of many nations, including the Mississaugas of the Credit, the Anishnabeg, the Chippewa, the Haudenosaunee, and the Wendat peoples, and is now home to many diverse First Nations, Inuit, and Métis peoples. We acknowledge that Toronto is covered by Treaty 13 with the Mississaugas of the Credit. We are grateful to live and work on this land.

Edited by Ian Williams
Cover design by Crystal Sikma, cover art by Lorna Livey
Interior design by Adam Haiun
Author photo by Holly Vestad

Coach House Books
80 bpNichol Lane
Toronto ON M5S 3J4
Canada

mail@chbooks.com
www.chbooks.com